Earthquake!

Introduction

Welcome to Half and Half books, a great combination of story and facts! You might want to read this book on your own. However, the section with real facts is a little more difficult to read than the story. You might find it helpful to read the facts section with your parent, or someone else, who can help you with the more difficult words. Your parent may also be able to answer any questions you have about the facts—or at least help you find more information!

Earthquake!

With special thanks to Malcolm Barker, author of *Three Fearful Days: San Francisco Memoirs of the 1906 Earthquake & Fire,* for his review and suggestions on the fiction portion of this book (Shaken to the Ground).

With special thanks to Eric Geist, Research Geophysicist, at the U.S. Geological Survey for his review and recommendations on the nonfiction portion of this book.

Printed in Singapore

Library of Congress Catalog Card Number: 2010921696

Hardcover ISBN: 978-1-60115-217-6
Paperback ISBN: 978-1-60115-218-3

Visit us online at:
www.HalfAndHalfBooks.com

EARTHQUAKE!

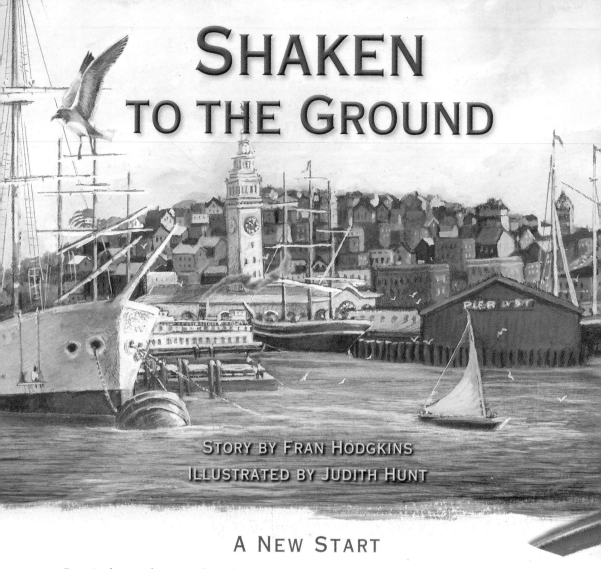

SHAKEN
TO THE GROUND

STORY BY FRAN HODGKINS

ILLUSTRATED BY JUDITH HUNT

A NEW START

Louis leaned over the ship's rail and gazed excitedly at the skyline. "San Francisco at last!" he said.

Dr. George Cabot grinned at his son and put his arm around his wife. "It's a wonderful sight after all these weeks at sea," the doctor said.

"I must say, it doesn't look like a frontier town at all," said Mrs. Cabot. "I'll have to write to Mrs. Emerson and tell her she's mistaken."

Dr. Cabot chuckled. "After all, frontier towns don't often have large hospitals that hire doctors from Massachusetts."

As the ship drew near the dock, Louis said to himself, "I hope San Francisco will be exciting!" He tried to take in all the activity on the pier. Voices spoke English, French, Spanish, Chinese, and other languages he could only guess at. Longshoremen unloaded the ship. Quickly they littered the dock with cargo of all sizes and shapes. Louis carried a small suitcase, while his father carried his medical satchel. Everything else they owned was inside trunks and crates that were somewhere among the jumble on the pier.

A tall, dark-haired young man held a sign that read "Dr. Cabot." Louis's father stopped and said, "I'm Dr. Cabot."

"Sir, what a pleasure to meet you. My name is Thomas Winter. I'm here to take you to the hotel where you'll be staying until your house is ready." The young fellow smiled. Louis instantly liked him. His father shook Thomas's hand and made introductions. "This is my wife and our son, Louis."

"Welcome to San Francisco," Thomas said as he took the suitcase and led the family to a car. "I'll come back and get your trunks after I drop you off."

"Would you like to sit up front, Louis?" Dr. Cabot asked. Louis nodded, and his parents settled into the back seat.

"What's that?" Louis asked, pointing at a large building. "That's the Ferry Building," Thomas said. "You can catch a boat there to Oakland and Berkeley." Thomas grinned. "They've got a fine big university over there at Berkeley," he said.

"Does it have a medical school?" Dr. Cabot asked. "I'd like my son to follow in my footsteps one day."

5

Louis sighed softly. Although he was proud of his father, Louis did not want to be a doctor himself. While Thomas and Dr. Cabot chatted, Louis studied the many buildings that lined Market Street. It truly was hard to believe that the city was so new. It had every-thing a city needed. Banks, as stately as any bank in Boston, stood along the cobblestone street. People bustled in and out of the en-trances of offices and shops. Carriages, cars, and trolleys shared the streets, and people on foot and on bicycles dodged among them. Thomas explained, "Underground cables pull the trolleys up the hills, which are too steep for horses. That's why we call them cable cars. We've had to be quite creative when it comes to solving the challenges involved with building around here."

Holding on to her hat, Mrs. Cabot said, "Is it true, Thomas, that the city is only about sixty years old?"

"Yes'm," he said. "At first, it was just a little place called Yerba Buena. Then after gold was discovered, the city grew like a weed. Today more than 400,000 people call San Francisco home."

They soon arrived at the Palace Hotel. Thomas handed the suitcase to a bellhop and declined the tip that Dr. Cabot offered. "My uncle started the hospital," he said. "When he said you were coming, I offered to pick you up. It gave me a chance to show off my city. You'll find that San Francisco is a special place."

As his parents checked in, Louis investigated a display in the lobby. Titled "The Safest Hotel in California," the display featured a tiny model of the hotel. To his amazement, Louis read that California experienced earthquakes, mighty movements of the ground. However, the Palace Hotel was built with two-foot-thick, iron-reinforced walls. "No earthquake could destroy the Palace," the display boasted.

His father called, "Come now, Louis. Let's have our dinner." He left the display and followed his parents to the dining room.

Later, washed up and in his nightclothes, Louis lay in bed. Thinking about how interesting his new city was, he drifted off to sleep.

DISASTER

When Louis awoke, it was still dark. He kept thinking about seeing this new city. Unable to sleep, he dressed quietly and then sat in an armchair, staring out the window at the dark. His parents snored softly in their bed.

Suddenly the chair shook. The two beds danced across the floor, waking his parents. "What the dickens!" exclaimed Dr. Cabot. Mrs. Cabot's eyes were wide with fright. The overhead lamp swung wildly. Louis clung to the chair as it shimmied across the floor and struck the wall.

Over the next minute, the earthquake shook the city. Streets lurched up and down. Water and gas pipes snapped. Bricks and cobblestones flew. Chimneys disintegrated. Windows shattered. In kitchens, stoves fell, and burning coal and logs skittered over wood floors. Small fires sprang up everywhere.

Once the quake ended, the family dressed quickly and hurried downstairs. In the lobby, the manager told guests, "You're perfectly safe, ladies and gentlemen. The Palace Hotel is earthquake-proof."

"What about fire?" someone asked.

"We have our own water supplies, stored in tanks right

here at the hotel. Should anything occur, it will be dealt with swiftly and effectively," the manager said. People murmured to each other, reassured.

Dr. Cabot turned to his family. "I need to go. I'm sure there are people who need my help. Louis, get my bag, please."

Louis took the stairs two at a time to their hotel room. Day was just dawning, and the view out the window stopped him in his tracks. The beautiful city he had seen the night before lay in ruins.

Dozens of the buildings he had admired on their ride to the hotel had been reduced to huge piles of rubble. He tore himself away from the window, picked up his father's medical bag, and hurried back downstairs.

Thomas was there, talking with his parents. His face was drawn with worry. "Thank you, son," his father said, taking the bag. He looked into Louis's eyes gravely. "I may be gone for a while, son. Take care of your mother."

Louis watched the men hurry out the door to Thomas's car. His mother joined him and put her arm around his shoulders. "Well, Louis, let's see where we might be of help."

Together they left the hotel. Because bricks and other debris covered the sidewalks, they walked in the street. The silence was eerie. Louis's mother reached out and took his hand, as much to comfort herself as to reassure him.

For hours, Louis and his mother walked around the city, offering what help they could to wounded and frightened citizens. Around noon, they began heading back toward the Palace Hotel for some food and rest. Suddenly Louis heard a faint groan that slowly grew louder.

He glanced up to see the top of the wall toppling toward them. "Look out!" he cried and pushed his mother toward the other side of the street. Behind them, the groan became a roar as the wall fell. It sent up a storm of dirt and brick dust.

Coughing, Louis covered his eyes with his left hand and gripped his mother's arm with the other. After a few moments, he opened his eyes. His mother stood next to him, frightened but unhurt. Her clothes had been tinted dark maroon by the brick dust.

"Help me!" cried a man's voice. "Help!"

THE MOST TERRIBLE DAY

Through the clearing dust, Louis saw a man lying in the street. He had leaped out of the way just in time to avoid being crushed by the falling wall. "My arm!" the man gasped. "The pain!" His face was greenish.

"It's broken," Louis said.

"We need to splint it and get you to the hospital," Mrs. Cabot said. Louis dug through the rubble until he found a piece of wood about a foot and a half long. Meanwhile, Mrs. Cabot tore her jacket into strips.

"This is going to hurt," she warned the man.

He nodded and bit his lip. Louis held the arm straight as his mother tied it securely to the wooden splint. Color drained from the man's face as they worked but gradually came back. "That helps. Thank you."

Just then, a police officer came around the corner and rushed up to help. "Come with me, sir," he said. "I'll get you to the hospital." The officer turned to the Cabots. "Where are you folks headed?" When he heard they were headed back to the Palace Hotel, he shook his head. "Sorry, ma'am, but the Palace Hotel is on fire, and there is no chance of saving it."

"Oh, no! Everything we had was at the hotel," exclaimed

Mrs. Cabot. "We arrived last night and don't know anyone. Could I follow you to the hospital? My husband is a doctor there."

"I wouldn't advise that, ma'am. Fires are breaking out all over the city. There is a chance the entire city is going to burn to the ground. I'd strongly advise you two to head over to the waterfront and catch one of the ferries out of town to someplace safe. I'll get word to your husband if you'd like."

"But how will he know where we are?"

"I heard that they're setting up a refugee camp in Berkeley," the officer said.

"Then we shall go there. Can you please get word to Dr. Edward
Cabot at the hospital, and let him know where we are?"

The officer repeated the name and tipped his hat. "Yes, ma'am, I'll
take this gentleman to see him right now. Best be getting along now."

Although he was frightened, Louis did not let it show. He looked
at his mother's calm face and realized that she too was hiding her
fear. He could tell by the tight lines around her mouth. He took her
hand and she smiled at him.

Dozens of people joined them as they traveled along Market Street. People picked their way over cracks in the street and around spots flooded by broken water mains. Snapped by the quake, power poles dangled by their electric lines.

They paused and surveyed the wreckage of a bank. Its huge safe had fallen through the floor and lay on its side in a deep hole. Several police officers stood on guard. "Move along, move along!" shouted one of the officers. "Nothing to see here!"

As they walked, the sky grew dark with ash. Fires burned throughout the city. No one knew it then, but gradually the fires would combine into one terrible raging firestorm. More than five hundred city blocks would be destroyed over the next four days.

The Cabots finally reached the Ferry Building. Crowds of people waited to board a boat and flee the city. Louis spied a sign that said Berkeley, and they joined the line of passengers. Soon after they boarded the ferry, it cast off from the dock.

CAMP

Like Louis and his mother, the other ferry passengers stood silently as they watched the fires burning throughout the city.

As they watched, Louis thought about the destruction. He could see that some buildings were standing almost intact. Most, though, had fallen. "How were they different?" he wondered. They all looked the same from the outside, but clearly something important was different between the buildings that still stood and those that had fallen. Was it the walls? The foundations? The ground they stood on?

Louis watched a little child with wide, frightened eyes clinging to her mother. The child reminded him of Ann, whose family had lived next door to them back in Boston. He liked Ann, and the thought of her being in a house that was collapsing made him angry. "Nobody should be scared about their house falling down," he said hotly, "especially a little child!"

As Louis raised his voice, people turned to look at him. His mother patted him on the hand and led him toward the bow.

"I'm sorry, Mother," he said. "Seeing the little girl so frightened upset me."

"I understand," she said. "Look, there's Berkeley." She pointed at the horizon. They watched it for a few minutes in silence.

At last, Louis said, "Remember how father always says one person can make a difference, and that's why he became a doctor? If I learned why these buildings fell, maybe I could help make better ones—ones that could stand up to earthquakes, like the hotel did."

His mother said, "Your father's heart is set on your being a doctor, you know."

"I know," he said. Feeling brave, he added, "But I don't want to."

"I know," replied Mrs. Cabot.

"You do?" he asked.

She smiled again. "Louis Cabot, I am your mother. If I didn't realize that you don't want to be a doctor, what kind of mother would I be? I've seen how you frown when he speaks of it."

Louis blushed. He thought he had hidden it so well!

"Now, don't you worry," his mother continued. "There's still plenty of time. We'll convince your father that medicine is not your calling."

Perhaps this disaster will show Father that medicine is not the only valuable career, Louis thought.

When the ferry docked, the passengers worked their way down the ferry's gangplank. No one pushed or shoved; it was all amazingly peaceful, as if everyone were out for a day trip rather than evacuating a city. A man bellowed, "Welcome to Berkeley, ladies and gentlemen! This way, if you please!"

The crowd of ferry passengers assembled around him. "Welcome to Berkeley, our neighbors from San Francisco! I am Professor Roberts, and I represent the university. With me today are dozens of my fellow faculty members and our students. We are here to help you get settled in temporary shelters that have been set up. Look for a person with an armband like mine, and he will be your chaperone." He lowered the megaphone to point at the red ribbon he wore around his upper right arm.

Groups of men with red armbands began taking people in small groups away from the crowd. They piled into automobiles, carriages, and wagons.

Louis and his mother waited their turn and were surprised when their chaperone turned out to be Professor Roberts himself. With a family of six, they climbed into a horse-drawn wagon. The professor took up the reins and off they went.

Louis sat close behind his mother, who was seated next to the professor. Mrs. Cabot asked, "How long have you been with the university, Professor Roberts?"

"Two and a half years now," he answered. "We hope our university will soon become equal to the fine colleges of the East."

Mrs. Cabot said, "What do you teach?"

"I am a professor in the college of civil engineering. One of my special research projects is investigating why certain buildings are more resistant to earthquakes than others."

"You mean, you're trying to find out why certain buildings stand up while others fall down?" Louis asked.

Professor Roberts smiled. "That's the gist of it, yes," he said. "Is that something that interests you?"

"Very much, sir," said Louis as the wagon rounded a curve into a large field. Throughout the field, groups of people were struggling to put up large canvas tents. Many more tents were flat on the ground, looking like huge puddles of fabric.

The professor slowed the horses. They stopped at a tent. "This will be temporary shelter for you," explained Professor Roberts. He helped Mrs. Cabot down from the seat of the wagon. The other family's four children had tumbled off like puppies and were happily chasing each other around as their parents took their bags from the wagon. Louis, feeling adventurous again, jumped off the wagon and landed on his feet next to his mother.

"Please excuse me, for others are waiting. However, I'll be back soon, and we can talk more," said Professor Roberts. They thanked him. He climbed back into the seat of the wagon, took up the reins, and headed back to the pier for more evacuees.

Louis and his mother entered the tent. It was furnished with three folding cots, each with a woolen blanket. "Home sweet home," she said.

MAKING A DIFFERENCE

Louis asked his mother. "May I look around?"

"Of course, Louis." She kissed him on the cheek, and he left the tent.

For a little while, Louis wandered about. He joined a crew that was setting up the tents, but his job was quickly taken over by some university students who were eager to help. Finally, on the other side of the camp, he came to a large oak tree. Under the tree, a girl about Louis's age was doing her best to keep a group of toddlers amused. The children were either crying or wandering off. Louis turned a small child around and led him back to the tree.

"Thank you," the girl said to Louis. "This is like trying to herd bees."

Louis chuckled as he replied, "You're welcome, miss. I'm glad to help out."

"My name is Emily Roberts," the young girl said as she quickly wrangled another wandering child.

"Are you Professor Roberts's daughter?" asked Louis.

"I am! Do you know Papa?"

"Yes. He drove us here on a wagon. My name is Louis Cabot."

"Oh," she said. "You're Dr. Cabot's son! Your father just arrived with some injured children from San Francisco. My papa is helping him set up a medical tent here."

"My father is here? In Berkeley?" asked Louis excitedly. Emily nodded and Louis raced off, calling back over his shoulder, "Excuse me, please! I must tell my mother!"

A short time later, Louis and his mother were anxiously searching the camp for the medical tent. After just a few minutes, Louis spotted a large tent with a big red cross. "There it is," he shouted.

As he and his mother approached, Dr. Cabot and Professor Roberts emerged from inside. "Father!" Louis cried as he ran to throw his arms around his waist. Dr. Cabot hugged his wife and son tightly, grateful that his family was safe and together once more.

Several weeks later, Louis and his father stood atop Telegraph Hill and looked down at the devastated city. Louis's mind was racing with questions and theories about why some buildings were still standing, while some were nothing but rubble. Suddenly his thoughts were interrupted by his father's voice. "There must be a way to prevent this devastation from ever happening again," his father said. "Perhaps someday you'll help provide some solutions, Louis. If you go to the university, you could start by taking some engineering classes with Professor Roberts."

Louis looked at his father questioningly. "But . . . I thought you wanted me to be a doctor."

Dr. Cabot smiled down at him. "I do. But you are much more interested in learning how to construct better buildings."

"How did you know, Father?"

Dr. Cabot put his arm around Louis's shoulder. "I'm your father, Louis Cabot. There aren't many secrets you can keep from me. Now let's go home. It's time to start rebuilding this great city of San Francisco."

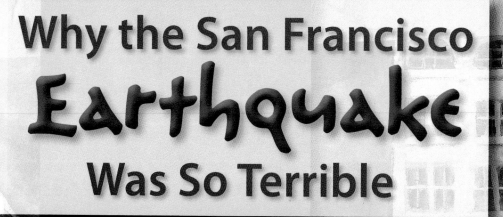

Why the San Francisco Earthquake Was So Terrible

The San Francisco earthquake of 1906 was one of the strongest earthquakes Americans have ever experienced. Why was it so terrible?

Wednesday 5:00 AM
San Francisco awakes

5:13 AM
Earthquake!

Much of the city was still asleep when the huge quake struck early on April 18, 1906. The main temblor only lasted about one minute, but the ground continued to shudder from aftershocks.

9:00 AM
Fires break out

Many buildings crumbled to the ground. Fires broke out all around the city and eventually joined to create one huge inferno that lasted for four days. Over 225,000 people were left homeless and 3,000 died, making this one of the worst natural disasters in the history of the United States.

Many parts of the city were built on former marshes that had been filled in with sand and other debris. This "made land" was very unstable and turned to mush during the earthquake—something called *liquefaction*. The soft, soggy ground could no longer support the buildings and many of them simply collapsed.

The shifting of the earth during the quake caused underground pipes to rupture. Some of those pipes carried natural gas, a highly flammable fuel. The leaking gas caused fires. Other broken pipes were water mains—and when the mains broke, that meant that firefighters had no water to use to fight the fires. Unchecked, the fires spread quickly.

Imagine a total disruption of your everyday life: Your house is too dangerous to live in, so you sleep on the sidewalk or in the front yard. You can't go inside to cook, so your parents grill on the street. There is no running water, so you can't get a drink, wash, or use the toilet. These were the experiences of many families after the 1906 earthquake.

Life in the Camps

The city, the U.S. Army, and others worked quickly to help the victims of the quake. Camps were set up, providing thousands of tents to serve as temporary houses.

Before long, the city replaced the tents with 6,000 small cottages. Some people liked the cottages so much that they lived there for years. A few of these tiny homes still survive, and you can see them in San Francisco.

The camps were great mixing bowls, as people from all economic levels and various backgrounds were thrown together. In the camps, the differences created by wealth (or the lack of it) disappeared. Everyone, no matter how rich or privileged they may have been before the quake, had to wait in line for food.

In spite of the total devastation of the 1906 earthquake, the people of San Francisco were determined to rebuild their city. A mere nine years later, the city hosted the Pan Pacific International Exposition to show the world it had recovered.

Understanding EARTHQUAKES

To understand why earthquakes like the one in San Francisco happen, we first must examine the ground beneath our feet.

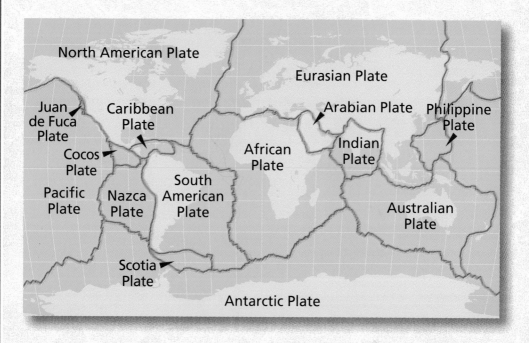

North American Plate

Eurasian Plate

Juan de Fuca Plate

Caribbean Plate

Arabian Plate

Philippine Plate

Cocos Plate

African Plate

Indian Plate

Pacific Plate

Nazca Plate

South American Plate

Australian Plate

Scotia Plate

Antarctic Plate

Wherever you stand, whether on a tall mountain or a sandy beach, the Earth's surface seems steady and solid. However, it is not one solid piece. It is actually made up of many pieces—pieces that are so huge that we aren't aware of their existence as we go about our day. The pieces are bigger than states, countries, even continents. They're called *tectonic plates*. They fit together and cover the entire surface of the earth—even the parts that are underwater.

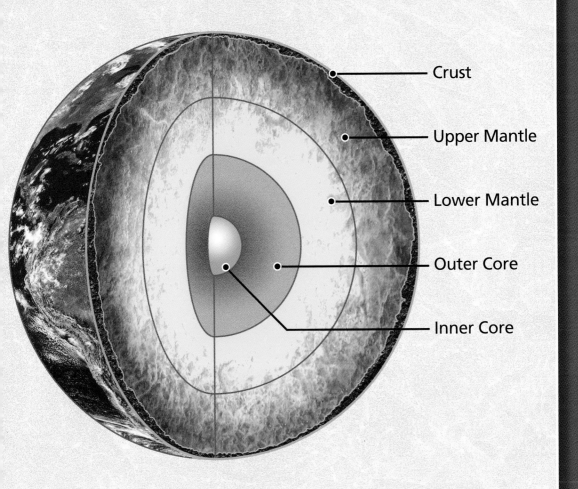

Crust

Upper Mantle

Lower Mantle

Outer Core

Inner Core

These plates are composed of the crust and the upper part of the Earth's mantle. The plates float on the lower mantle, which completely surrounds the planet's dense, hot core.

Because the lower mantle is extremely hot, it is always moving. And as the lower mantle moves, it drags the plates along with it.

How Plates Fit Together

Scientists call the places where two plates meet a *plate boundary.* *Boundary* is another word for "edge." Three main kinds of plate boundaries exist: convergent, divergent, and transform.

A lot of geologic activity takes place at plate boundaries. As one plate collides with another, they may both wrinkle into mountains. One may be forced under the other. Volcanoes and earthquakes occur most often at or near plate boundaries.

When two plates are moving toward each other, they form a **convergent boundary.** **Converge** means move together.

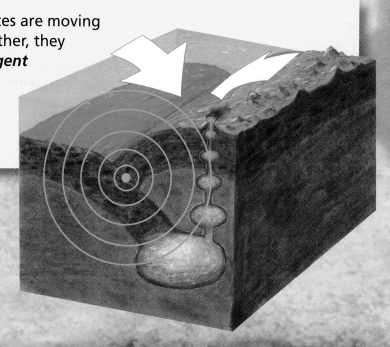

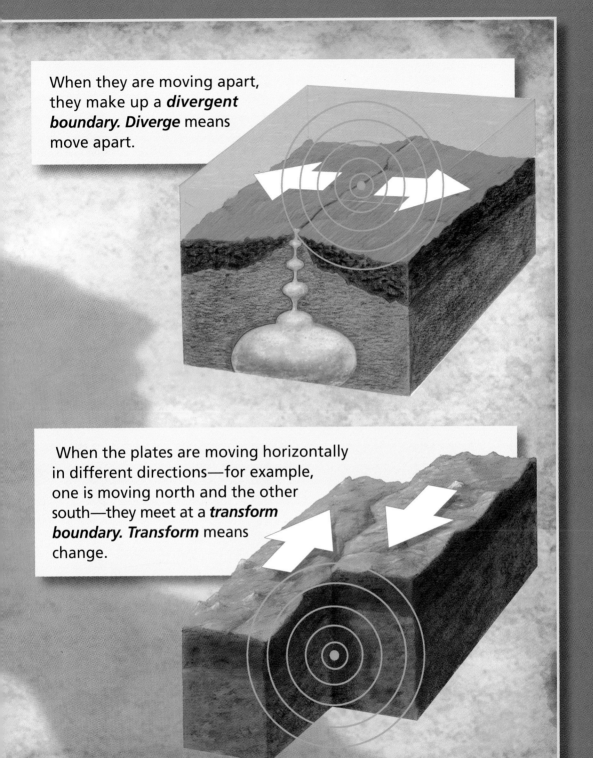

When they are moving apart, they make up a **divergent boundary. Diverge** means move apart.

When the plates are moving horizontally in different directions—for example, one is moving north and the other south—they meet at a **transform boundary. Transform** means change.

How Earthquakes Happen

The plates of the Earth move about as fast as your fingernails grow. However, sometimes the plates get "stuck" and don't move at all for a period of time. Pressure builds. Then suddenly they move very quickly.

San Andreas Fault, Carrizo Plain, California.

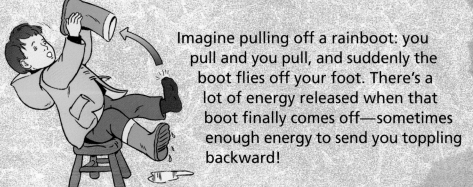

Imagine pulling off a rainboot: you pull and you pull, and suddenly the boot flies off your foot. There's a lot of energy released when that boot finally comes off—sometimes enough energy to send you toppling backward!

The same thing happens after plates have been grinding against each other for many years. At some point, the energy is released in a sudden, explosive event: an earthquake.

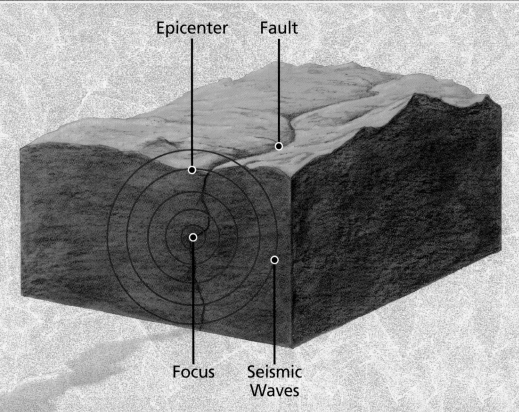

Epicenter   Fault

Focus   Seismic
Waves

The point where an earthquake begins is called its *focus*. The focus of an earthquake may be near the surface, or it may be as deep as 400 miles underground. The point on the Earth's surface directly over the focus is called the *epicenter*.

The energy of an earthquake travels out from the focus in the form of *seismic* (sīz′ mik) *waves*. The seismic waves of an earthquake release great amounts of energy in a short amount of time— usually in less than a minute. After an earthquake, lesser quakes called *aftershocks* are common.

The Magnitude of
EARTHQUAKES

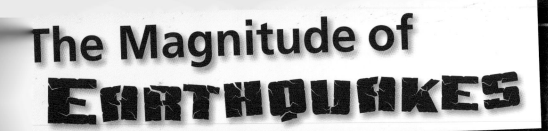

Magnitude is the way that scientists measure the amount of energy released by an earthquake.

The magnitude scale for earthquakes is based on mathematical formulas called *logarithms*. On the magnitude scale, each whole number reflects 10 times the intensity and 31 times the energy of the previous number. Therefore, a quake of 6.0 is actually 10 times more intense and releases 31 times the energy of a quake of 5.0.

The San Francisco earthquake of 1906 is estimated to have had a magnitude of 7.8.

Quake Magnitude Scale

| 2.0 – 4.9 | 5.0 – 5.9 | 6.0 – 6.9 | 7.0 – 7.9 | 8.0+ |

- A quake that registers less than 2.0 on the magnitude scale is called a microquake and would probably not be felt by humans.

- Quakes between 2.0 and 4.9 might be felt but would probably not cause much damage.

- Quakes between 5.0 and 5.9 are considered "moderate" and could cause damage to poorly constructed buildings.

- Quakes between 6.0 and 6.9 are likely to be felt by everyone in the area and can be destructive.

- Quakes between 7.0 and 7.9 are considered to be major earth-quakes and can cause serious damage over large areas.

- Quakes of 8.0 and above are considered "great" earthquakes, and their damage can be devastating.

Some Effects of Earthquakes

The effects of an earthquake vary widely, depending on the magnitude.

During a small earthquake, the shaking may just feel like a big truck is driving by. In a moderate earthquake, windows may shatter and pictures might fall off walls. In a large earthquake, walls, chimneys, and brick buildings may fall. Major earthquakes can cause large cracks to appear in the ground and often cause major damage to poorly constructed buildings.

Liquefaction

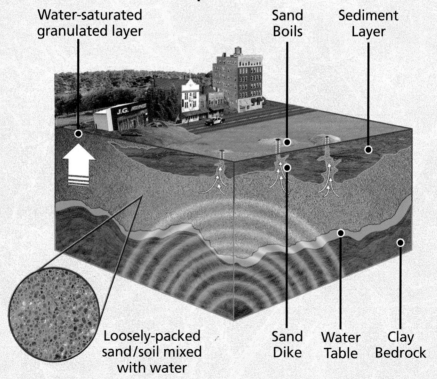

Water-saturated granulated layer

Sand Boils

Sediment Layer

Loosely-packed sand/soil mixed with water

Sand Dike

Water Table

Clay Bedrock

Sometimes a building will collapse due to liquefaction, which occurs when the loosely-packed, wet soil underneath it is shaken so hard that it takes on a pudding-like or liquid-like consistency. When the ground turns soft, it can't support the buildings, and the buildings sink.

Liquefaction is responsible for much of the damage sustained in the Marina district of San Francisco during the Loma Prieta earthquake of 1989. That earthquake had a magnitude between 6.9 and 7.1.

During the 1906 earthquake, liquefaction caused a four-story hotel to sink so deep that only the fourth floor remained above ground!

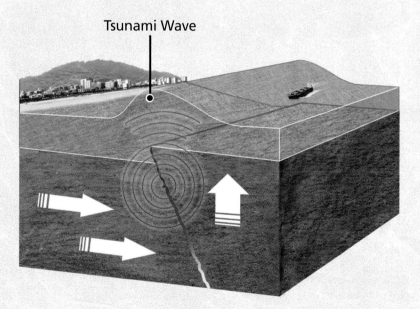

Tsunami Wave

Tsunamis are another deadly effect of earthquakes. These huge waves occur when an undersea earthquake lifts up part of the sea bed. The movement creates a huge wave which can travel for thousands of miles. When it approaches the shore, the tsunami gets higher, reaching as much as 30 meters (100 feet) into the air.

Other Famous Earthquakes

Alaska, 1964

Alaska and California have the most earthquakes of all the states. On March 28, 1964, Alaska experienced the second-largest earthquake ever recorded, measuring 9.2 on the magnitude scale. More than 100 people died, most of them from the tsunami that struck the state.

Tokyo, Japan 1923

On September 1, 1923, an earthquake of magnitude 7.9–8.3 occurred near Tokyo, Japan. The powerful earthquake immediately destroyed a huge number of buildings. The quake also struck just before noon when many people were cooking their lunch over open flames, resulting in a devastating firestorm. In addition, the earthquake created 30-foot tsunami waves that caused destructive floods.

Banda Aceh, Indonesia 2004

The Banda Aceh earthquake occurred far out at sea under the Indian Ocean and measured 9.1 on the magnitude scale. The tsunami waves it generated caused the deaths of thousands of people in Sri Lanka, India, Indonesia, and other coastal nations. After the tide rushed out, the waves came in, washing over everything in their path.

Make a Model to Simulate an Earthquake

How do you study something that you can't predict? Scientists who study earthquakes and engineers who design earthquake-resistant structures use models. They create "model" earthquakes by using a device called a shake plate. The shake plate simulates the multi-directional movement the Earth experiences during a quake.

You can build your own model shake plate.

What you need:
- A shallow pan, like a cookie sheet
- Enough marbles to cover the cookie sheet
- A sheet of cardboard
- A model structure to test

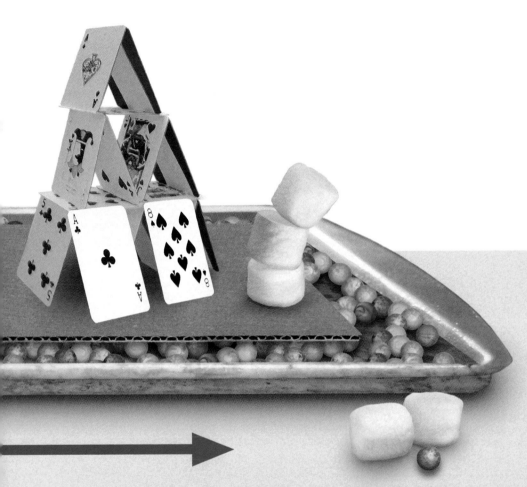

1. Place the marbles in a single layer on the cookie sheet.

2. Put the cardboard on top of the marbles.

3. Build a structure to test on top of the marbles.

4. Shake the pan from side to side. What happens to your structure?

Experiment with different materials and ways of building your structures to see what works best—for example, marshmallows stacked on top of each other and marshmallows stacked but attached with toothpicks.

Building Better Buildings

Scientists and engineers realized that the great city of San Francisco would have been safer if there had been better engineering design applied to its buildings. However, it would be another 19 years—and another quake—before revised building codes would be in place. And that was in a different city altogether! The city of Santa Barbara instituted the nation's first earthquake building code after an earthquake struck there in 1925.

The materials used to construct a building and how a building is constructed can make a big difference in whether it will survive a big earthquake. Buildings made of brick are often very vulnerable, particularly if the brickwork is not reinforced with metal. Steel and wood are usually better construction materials because they can flex more as a building moves during a quake. Brickwork doesn't flex as easily, so it is more likely to crumble when shaken hard.

Elastomeric Isolator
Rubber and steel plates with lead core

Steel Seismic Damper

Lead Seismic Damper

Another way to help protect buildings from earthquakes is to build them on *shake pads*, or *isolators*. These structures act like shock absorbers in a car. When the ground moves, the part of the shake pad or isolator attached to the ground moves with it. The other part, which is attached to the building, doesn't move. (Smaller versions of shake pads keep washing machines from bouncing across the floor.)

Modern earthquake building codes require buildings to have safe and effective evacuation routes. Elevators and electric doors may not work after an earthquake, so there must be other ways to leave the building.

Predicting Earthquakes

Wouldn't it be great if we could tell when an earthquake was coming so we could get out of the way?

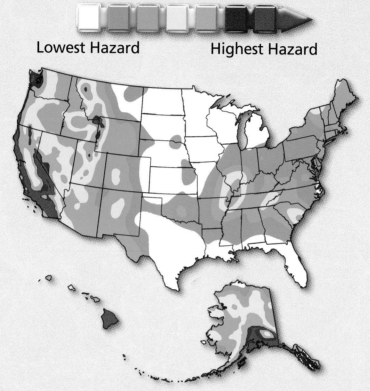

Lowest Hazard   Highest Hazard

At this time, scientists can't predict earthquakes. However, they can compile earthquake hazard maps, based on past data. These maps show the places where earthquakes are most likely to occur. In the United States, earthquake hot spots include the West Coast, Alaska and Hawaii. South Carolina is a hot spot on the East Coast. On the other hand, Florida, most of Texas, and the upper Midwest (including Minnesota, Michigan, and Wisconsin), have a low risk of earthquakes.

However, "low risk" doesn't mean "no risk." We can base plans for the future on what has happened in the past, but no one can ever predict what will happen with 100 percent accuracy.

Be Prepared

It is always a good idea to be prepared in case an earthquake or another natural disaster strikes.

Before an Earthquake

Gather supplies. Make sure you have enough food and water for each family member—including your pets—for at least three days. And remember: the power may be out, so you probably won't be able to microwave anything, use an electric can opener, or cook with your stove!

Have a flashlight and a radio with batteries (or one that has a hand crank and doesn't need batteries).

Put a pair of shoes, long pants, and a long-sleeved shirt in a place that you can easily find in the dark (such as in a bag tied to a leg of your bed).

During and After an Earthquake

During an Earthquake

If you are indoors, quickly climb under a sturdy desk or table. Hang on tight! If you are outdoors, stay there, but stay away from power lines. Drop to the ground and don't try to run.

After an Earthquake

Check and make sure you aren't hurt. If you are injured, do first aid or get help. If you are in your pajamas, put on shoes, long pants, and a shirt with long sleeves. These will protect you from being cut by broken objects.

First Aid Kit

If you are separated from your family, plan to meet at a preselected meeting spot. Phone service may be out, so don't count on using your cell phone.

Check and make sure phones haven't gotten knocked off the hook; off-the-hook phones tie up phone service. Use phones only to call 911—and only if you have an urgent need for immediate assistance.

Follow directions of emergency personnel, and be ready to help your neighbors. Expect aftershocks.

Earthquakes are just one of the many natural disasters that may occur in your lifetime. Learning what to do in an emergency will help prepare you for whatever surprises nature may bring.

An Earthquake Quiz

1. True or False: California is the only U.S. state that experiences earthquakes.

2. Earthquakes happen when _____.
   a. a marble drops into a frog's mouth
   b. a huge ocean wave strikes the land
   c. tectonic plates move
   d. sea levels rise

3. The San Francisco earthquake was especially bad because _____
   a. the city had no postal service.
   b. part of the city was built on fill.
   c. the city received no outside help.
   d. no cable cars were in service.

4. After the earthquake, some San Franciscans were evacuated to which city?
   a. Los Angeles
   b. Sacramento
   c. Berkeley
   d. San Diego

5. How does a shake pad protect a building during an earthquake?
   a. It absorbs the quake's energy and keeps it from reaching the building.
   b. It diverts the energy of the quake into special water tanks.
   c. It changes the kinetic energy of the quake into heat energy.
   d. It makes the building shake more quickly than the ground does.

6. After the San Francisco Earthquake of 1906 many victims lived in _____.

   a. hotels
   b. burned-out buildings
   c. caves
   d. tents and cottages

7. True or False: South Carolina is one of the places in the United States at high risk for earthquake activity.

8. After the 1906 earthquake, most of San Francisco was destroyed by _____.

   a. flood
   b. winds
   c. fire
   d. snow

9. Which state has experienced a very large earthquake?

   a. Maryland
   b. Florida
   c. Michigan
   d. Alaska

10. If an earthquake hits, what should you do?

   a. Hide under a sturdy table.
   b. Run outdoors immediately.
   c. Hold your breath.
   d. Call the police for help.

Answers: 1. false: All states except North Dakota and Florida have had quakes; California and Alaska have had the most. 2. c, 3. b, 4. c, 5. a, 6. d, 7. true, 8. c, 9. d, 10. a